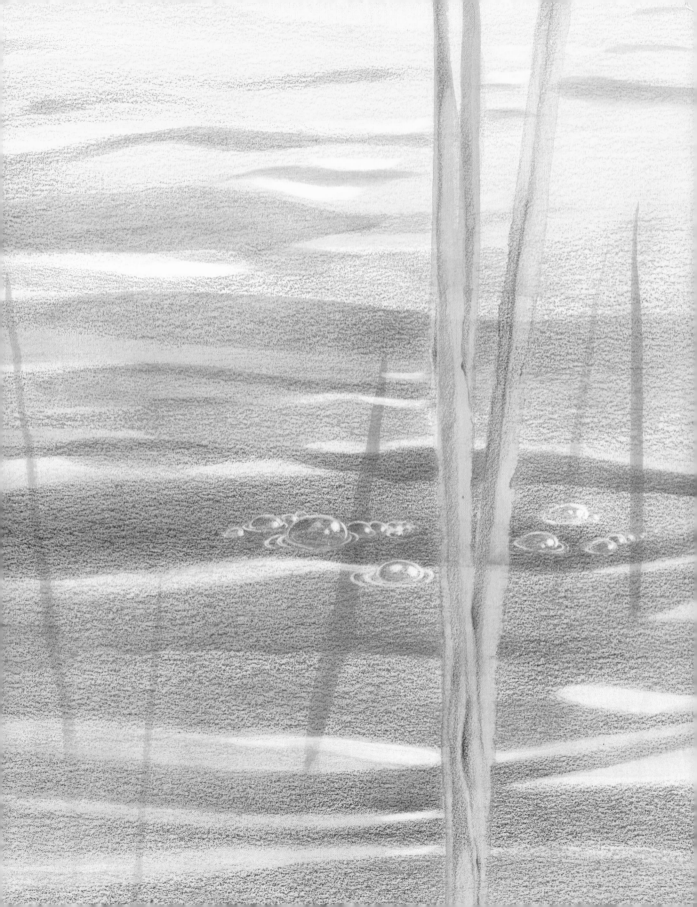

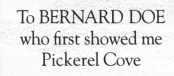

To BERNARD DOE
who first showed me
Pickerel Cove

Library of Congress Cataloging in Publication Data   Arnosky, Jim. Come out, muskrats. Summary: In late afternoon the muskrats come out to swim, dive, and eat green water weeds. 1. Muskrats—Juvenile literature.   [1. Muskrats] I. Title. QL737.R638A76 1989   599.32′33   88-26611   ISBN 0-688-05457-9   ISBN 0-688-05458-6 (lib. bdg.)

COME OUT, MUSKRATS

Jim Arnosky

Lothrop, Lee & Shepard Books
New York

In late afternoon
when the cove becomes calm

and tall cattails reflect in still water,

it's time for the muskrats
to come out of their house.
Come out, muskrats, come out.

Come out to swim in the shallows
and eat green water weeds.

Climb up on your house
and rub your fur dry.

Then dive in the water
and get wet again.

Swim between the lily pads.

Race around the cattails.

Go this way and that way—
through the setting sun.

When it gets dark and
the birds end their songs—

stay out, muskrats, stay out,

and swim until dawn.